# Awakening Your Inner Self: Lessons from BK Sister Shivani's Inspirational Talks

## C. P. Kumar
Reiki Healer
Roorkee - 247667, India

# DEDICATION

This book "Awakening Your Inner Self: Lessons from BK Sister Shivani's Inspirational Talks" is dedicated to BK Sister Shivani, a spiritual teacher and motivational speaker from India. She is a member of the Brahma Kumaris World Spiritual University and is well-known for her lectures on the topics of spirituality, self-transformation, and personal development. Sister Shivani's talks are based on the teachings of the Brahma Kumaris and emphasize the importance of meditation, positive thinking, and developing a deeper connection with the self and the Divine. Her soothing voice and practical wisdom have made her a beloved figure among millions of people worldwide who seek guidance on their spiritual journey.

Your wisdom, guidance, and inspiration have touched the lives of millions around the world. Your teachings on awakening our inner self have empowered us to find happiness, peace, and purpose in our lives. This book is dedicated to you, as a tribute to your incredible contribution to the field of spirituality. Your voice has been a beacon of hope for so many, and we hope that the lessons and insights shared within these pages will continue to inspire and guide countless others on their own journey of self-discovery. Thank you for your unwavering dedication and commitment to helping us awaken our inner selves.

**C. P. Kumar**

# CONTENTS

# PREFACE

We live in a fast-paced world where the demands of modern life often leave us feeling disconnected from our inner selves. In our quest for success and happiness, we sometimes lose sight of what truly matters in life - our inner peace, joy, and purpose.

In this book, we explore the teachings of BK Sister Shivani, a spiritual teacher and a renowned speaker, who has helped millions of people around the world to awaken their inner selves and transform their lives. Her inspiring talks and teachings provide a practical roadmap for personal growth and development, drawing on the wisdom of ancient spiritual traditions and making it accessible to modern audiences.

Through the chapters of this book, we delve into BK Sister Shivani's philosophy, and explore her teachings on inner awakening. We learn about the nature of the mind and its impact on our well-being, the power of positive thinking and affirmations, and the importance of self-awareness and mindfulness. We also discover the transformative power of letting go of negative emotions and cultivating forgiveness, and the role of spirituality in our inner transformation.

Furthermore, we explore the concept of finding purpose and meaning in life, and the importance of self-care and self-love in our journey towards self-realization. We learn how to overcome obstacles and challenges, and how to build harmonious relationships with others. Finally, we explore practical strategies for integrating spiritual practices into our daily lives, so that we can live a life that is aligned with our deepest values and aspirations.

This book is for anyone who is seeking to awaken their inner self and find greater meaning and purpose in life. It is a guide for those who want to live a more fulfilling and joyful life, and who are willing to explore the wisdom of ancient spiritual traditions in order to achieve this goal.

We hope that this book will serve as a source of inspiration and guidance for all those who are on the path to self-realization, and that it will help readers to awaken their inner selves and transform their lives in a positive and meaningful way.

C. P. Kumar

# Chapter 1. BK Sister Shivani's Journey and Philosophy

## Introduction

BK Sister Shivani is a spiritual teacher, motivational speaker, and a leading light of the Brahma Kumaris, a global spiritual movement based in India. Sister Shivani's teachings have touched the hearts and minds of millions of people worldwide, and her videos on YouTube have garnered over 85 million views. Her simple yet profound message of inner transformation and self-empowerment has inspired countless people to lead a more fulfilling life.

## Early Life

Sister Shivani was born in Pune, India, in 1972. Her birth name was Shivani Verma, and she grew up in a family that valued education and spiritual learning. Her father, Dr. Girish Verma, was a well-known scientist, and her mother, Dr. Kusum Verma, was a spiritual teacher who introduced Shivani to the Brahma Kumaris when she was in her early 20s.

Shivani studied electronics engineering at Pune University and worked as a lecturer at a college in Mumbai. However, she felt unfulfilled in her job and yearned for a deeper purpose in life. She turned to spirituality and began attending the Brahma Kumaris center in Mumbai, where she learned about meditation and the power of positive thinking.

## Journey with the Brahma Kumaris

Sister Shivani's journey with the Brahma Kumaris began in 1995 when she attended a 7-day meditation course. She found the teachings and the practice of meditation to be transformative, and she soon became a regular attendee of the center. She completed the 7-year course of spiritual study offered by the Brahma Kumaris and became a teacher in 2007.

Sister Shivani's teachings are based on the core principles of the Brahma Kumaris, which include the understanding that we are all spiritual beings having a human experience, that the quality of our thoughts and beliefs shapes our reality, and that true happiness and fulfillment come from within. She teaches that our thoughts are like seeds that we plant in our minds, and that we can choose to nurture positive thoughts and beliefs that lead to growth and transformation.

## Philosophy

Sister Shivani's philosophy is grounded in the belief that true transformation and happiness come from within. She teaches that we all have the power to create the life we desire, and that the key to doing so is to change our thoughts and beliefs. She emphasizes the importance of self-awareness and self-reflection, and teaches that the more we understand ourselves, the more we can transform ourselves.

One of Sister Shivani's most powerful teachings is the concept of karma. She explains that karma is not punishment or reward, but rather the consequences of our actions and thoughts. She teaches that the universe is like a mirror, reflecting back to us the energy and vibrations that we emit. By changing our thoughts and actions, we can change the energy that we send out into the universe, and thereby change our reality.

Sister Shivani also emphasizes the importance of cultivating a positive mindset. She teaches that our thoughts create our reality, and that we can choose to focus on the positive aspects of our lives rather than dwelling on the negative. She encourages her students to practice gratitude and to appreciate the blessings in their lives, no matter how small they may seem.

## Teachings

Sister Shivani's teachings are based on the belief that we are all spiritual beings having a human experience. She teaches that we are all interconnected, and that the quality of our thoughts and beliefs affects the world around us. She encourages her students to focus on inner transformation, rather than external achievement, and to cultivate qualities such as love, compassion, and forgiveness.

One of Sister Shivani's most popular teachings is the concept of "soul consciousness." She explains that soul consciousness is the state of being aware of oneself as a spiritual being, rather than just a physical body. She teaches that by cultivating soul consciousness, we can tap into our inner wisdom and guidance, and live a more purposeful and fulfilling life.

Sister Shivani also teaches the importance of meditation as a tool for inner transformation. She emphasizes that meditation is not just a technique, but a way of life. She teaches that through regular meditation practice, we can develop a deeper connection with our inner self and with the divine, and thereby access a source of inner peace and strength.

## Impact

Sister Shivani's teachings have had a profound impact on people from all walks of life. Her simple yet powerful message of self-transformation and empowerment has resonated with millions of people around the world. Her videos on YouTube have become a source of inspiration and guidance for many, and she has been featured in numerous media outlets, including The Times of India, The Huffington Post, and The Economic Times.

Sister Shivani has also been invited to speak at numerous conferences and events, including the United Nations International Day of Yoga, the World Parliament of Religions, and the Global Festival of Spiritual Sciences. Her talks and workshops have helped people from diverse backgrounds to connect with their inner self and to live a more fulfilling and purposeful life.

## Conclusion

Sister Shivani's journey and philosophy are a testament to the power of inner transformation and self-empowerment. Through her teachings, she has helped countless people to tap into their inner wisdom and guidance, and to live a life of purpose and meaning. Her message of love, compassion, and forgiveness has touched the hearts of millions of people around the world, and her impact continues to grow.

As Sister Shivani once said, "Happiness is not something that we get from outside, but something that we create from within." Her teachings remind us that true happiness and fulfillment come from within, and that by changing our thoughts and beliefs, we can transform our lives and the world around us.

## Introduction

BK Sister Shivani is a renowned spiritual
leader and teacher who has been inspiring
people to live a more conscious and
fulfilling life for many years. Her teachings
on inner awakening have helped countless
individuals to connect with their inner self,
find inner peace and live a more authentic
and fulfilling life. In this article, we will
explore some of the key teachings of BK
Sister Shivani and how they can help us in
our journey towards inner awakening.

## Understanding the Self

One of the fundamental teachings of BK
Sister Shivani is the importance of
understanding the self. According to her, we
need to take the time to reflect on who we
are, what our values and beliefs are, and
what our purpose in life is. This self-
reflection helps us to connect with our inner
self and understand our true potential. She
teaches that when we understand ourselves,
we are better equipped to deal with life's

challenges and make better decisions that align with our true selves.

## Meditation and Mindfulness

BK Sister Shivani emphasizes the importance of meditation and mindfulness in achieving inner awakening. Meditation is a powerful tool that can help us to quiet our minds, reduce stress and anxiety, and connect with our inner self. Mindfulness, on the other hand, is about being fully present in the moment and paying attention to our thoughts, feelings, and sensations without judgment. By practicing meditation and mindfulness regularly, we can develop a deeper sense of awareness and inner peace.

## Positive Thinking

Another key teaching of BK Sister Shivani is the power of positive thinking. She believes that our thoughts have a profound impact on our lives and that we can create our own reality through the power of our thoughts. By cultivating positive thoughts and focusing on what we want to achieve, we can attract positive experiences and opportunities into our lives. On the other hand, negative thoughts and self-talk can hold us back and create a self-fulfilling prophecy of failure.

## Letting Go of Attachments

BK Sister Shivani teaches that attachments to material possessions, people, and experiences can hold us back from experiencing true inner awakening. She encourages us to let go of our attachments and focus on what really matters in life. When we let go of attachments, we are able to connect with our inner selves and experience true freedom and happiness.

## Living with Purpose

Finally, BK Sister Shivani teaches the importance of living with purpose. She encourages us to identify our unique talents and passions and use them to make a positive impact in the world. When we live with purpose, we are able to find meaning and fulfillment in our lives, and we can make a difference in the lives of others. By living with purpose, we are able to connect with our inner selves and experience true inner awakening.

# Conclusion

BK Sister Shivani's teachings on inner awakening have inspired millions of people around the world to connect with their inner selves, find inner peace, and live a more authentic and fulfilling life. By understanding the self, practicing meditation and mindfulness, cultivating positive thoughts, letting go of attachments, and living with purpose, we can experience true inner awakening and live our best lives. Whether you are just starting on your spiritual journey or have been practicing for many years, BK Sister Shivani's teachings can help you to deepen your understanding of yourself, connect with your inner self, and live a more meaningful and fulfilling life.

## Introduction

The mind is a fascinating and complex aspect of our being that has long been a topic of interest and study in various fields such as psychology, philosophy, and spirituality. Understanding the nature of the mind and its impact on our well-being is crucial for leading a fulfilling life. In this article, we will explore BK Sister Shivani's perspective on the nature of the mind and how it impacts our well-being.

## Understanding the Nature of the Mind

According to BK Sister Shivani, the mind is like a garden that needs to be tended to regularly. Just as a gardener must weed, prune, and water the garden to keep it healthy, we must also take care of our minds to maintain our well-being. The mind is not just the physical brain, but it includes our thoughts, feelings, and emotions. Our thoughts are like seeds that we plant in our minds, and they can grow into positive or negative emotions depending on how we nurture them.

BK Sister Shivani believes that our minds are powerful tools that can shape our lives. Our thoughts create our reality, and what we focus on grows. If we focus on negative thoughts and emotions, we will attract negative experiences into our lives. On the other hand, if we focus on positive thoughts and emotions, we will attract positive experiences.

## The Impact of the Mind on Our Well-Being

The mind has a significant impact on our well-being, both physical and mental. Our thoughts and emotions can affect our health, relationships, and overall quality of life. Negative thoughts and emotions can lead to stress, anxiety, and depression, which can cause physical symptoms such as headaches, fatigue, and digestive issues.

BK Sister Shivani emphasizes the importance of cultivating positive thoughts and emotions to improve our well-being.

She teaches that our thoughts and emotions are like vibrations that radiate out into the world and affect those around us. If we cultivate positive thoughts and emotions, we can create a positive ripple effect that will benefit not only ourselves but also those around us.

## Techniques for Cultivating a Positive Mindset

BK Sister Shivani teaches various techniques for cultivating a positive mindset, such as meditation, positive affirmations, and visualization. Meditation is a powerful tool for quieting the mind and reducing stress. It can help us gain clarity and insight into our thoughts and emotions, which can lead to a more positive outlook on life.

Positive affirmations are another technique that BK Sister Shivani recommends for cultivating a positive mindset. Affirmations are positive statements that we repeat to ourselves to reinforce positive beliefs and attitudes. For example, we might repeat the affirmation, "I am strong, capable, and worthy," to boost our confidence and self-esteem.

Visualization is another technique that BK Sister Shivani uses to help people cultivate a positive mindset. Visualization involves creating a mental image of a desired outcome or experience. For example, if we want to improve our relationships, we might visualize ourselves having loving and supportive interactions with our loved ones.

## Conclusion

Understanding the nature of the mind and its impact on our well-being is crucial for leading a fulfilling life. BK Sister Shivani's perspective on the mind highlights the importance of cultivating positive thoughts and emotions to maintain our well-being. Negative thoughts and emotions can lead to physical and mental health issues, while positive thoughts and emotions can create a positive ripple effect in our lives and those around us. Techniques such as meditation, positive affirmations, and visualization can help us cultivate a positive mindset and improve our overall quality of life. It is essential to tend to our minds like a garden and nurture it regularly for a healthy and fulfilling life.

## Introduction

The power of positive thinking and
affirmations has been acknowledged for
centuries. Our thoughts have a profound
impact on our lives, and what we believe,
we become. This concept has been
beautifully explained by BK Sister Shivani,
an Indian spiritual teacher and motivational
speaker. Sister Shivani has been spreading
her message of positivity and spiritual
awakening across the world through her
talks, books, and TV shows. In this article,
we will delve into Sister Shivani's
perspective on the power of positive
thinking and affirmations and how it can
transform our lives.

## What is Positive Thinking?

Positive thinking is the practice of
cultivating positive thoughts and emotions.
It involves focusing on the good in any
situation and looking for the silver lining.

Positive thinking is not just about ignoring the negative aspects of life, but it is about reframing them in a positive light. Positive thinking can have a significant impact on our mental and physical well-being, relationships, and success in life.

## The Power of Positive Thinking

According to Sister Shivani, our thoughts create our reality. Our thoughts are like seeds, and what we plant in our minds will grow and manifest in our lives. Positive thoughts create positive outcomes, while negative thoughts create negative outcomes. She stresses that we must choose our thoughts carefully because they shape our reality.

Sister Shivani believes that we can train our minds to think positively. It requires conscious effort to replace negative thoughts with positive ones. She recommends starting the day with positive affirmations that set the tone for the day ahead. She suggests saying affirmations like "Today is going to be a great day" or "I am capable of achieving my goals" to create a positive mindset.

# Affirmations

Affirmations are positive statements that we repeat to ourselves to reprogram our subconscious mind. The subconscious mind is where our beliefs and habits are stored, and it controls our behavior. By repeating positive affirmations, we can replace negative beliefs with positive ones.

Sister Shivani stresses the importance of affirmations in creating a positive mindset. She believes that affirmations can help us overcome limiting beliefs and negative self-talk. She recommends creating affirmations that resonate with us personally and repeating them daily.

Examples of positive affirmations include "I am worthy and deserving of love and respect," "I trust in the universe to guide me towards my highest good," and "I am confident in my abilities and talents."

## The Impact of Positive Thinking and Affirmations

Sister Shivani believes that positive thinking and affirmations can transform our lives in many ways. Here are some of the ways in which she believes they can have an impact:

1. Improved Mental Health: Positive thinking and affirmations can improve our mental health by reducing stress and anxiety. By focusing on positive thoughts, we can create a more peaceful and calm mindset.

2. Increased Resilience: Positive thinking and affirmations can increase our resilience and help us bounce back from setbacks. By believing in ourselves and our abilities, we can overcome challenges and achieve our goals.

3. Improved Relationships: Positive thinking and affirmations can improve our relationships by creating a more positive and loving energy. When we believe in ourselves and our worth, we attract positive and supportive relationships.

4. Increased Success: Positive thinking and affirmations can increase our success by creating a mindset of abundance and possibility. By believing in ourselves and our potential, we can achieve our goals and manifest our desires.

# Conclusion

Positive thinking and affirmations are powerful tools that can transform our lives. As explained by Sister Shivani, our thoughts shape our reality, and by choosing to focus on positivity and repeating affirmations, we can reprogram our minds to believe in ourselves and our potential. The impact of positive thinking and affirmations can be seen in many aspects of our lives, including improved mental health, increased resilience, improved relationships, and increased success. By incorporating these practices into our daily lives, we can create a more fulfilling and joyful life.

# Chapter 5. Developing Self-awareness and Mindfulness

## Introduction

Self-awareness and mindfulness are essential components of personal growth and spiritual development. In recent years, the practice of mindfulness has gained widespread popularity, with many people seeking to incorporate this practice into their daily lives. BK Sister Shivani is a renowned spiritual leader who has been instrumental in spreading awareness about the benefits of mindfulness and self-awareness. In this article, we will explore her perspective on developing self-awareness and mindfulness and how these practices can positively impact our lives.

## What is self-awareness?

Self-awareness is the ability to recognize and understand our emotions, thoughts, and behavior. It is an essential component of emotional intelligence and helps us to develop better relationships with ourselves and others. When we are self-aware, we can identify our strengths and weaknesses and make informed decisions about our lives. Self-awareness is not something that comes naturally to most people; it requires intentional effort and practice.

## BK Sister Shivani's perspective on self-awareness

According to BK Sister Shivani, self-awareness is the key to personal growth and spiritual development. She believes that developing self-awareness requires a deep understanding of our thoughts, emotions, and behavior. To become more self-aware, we need to take the time to reflect on our experiences and understand the underlying emotions that drive our behavior.

BK Sister Shivani also emphasizes the importance of self-acceptance in developing self-awareness. She believes that when we accept ourselves for who we are, including our flaws and imperfections, we can begin to work on improving ourselves. Self-acceptance allows us to be honest with ourselves about our strengths and weaknesses, and this honesty is the foundation of self-awareness.

# What is mindfulness?

Mindfulness is the practice of being present in the moment and paying attention to our thoughts, emotions, and sensations without judgment. It is a form of meditation that helps us to become more aware of our thoughts and emotions and develop a greater sense of self-awareness. Mindfulness is not just about being present in the moment; it is also about cultivating a sense of compassion and empathy towards ourselves and others.

## BK Sister Shivani's perspective on mindfulness

According to BK Sister Shivani, mindfulness is a powerful tool for personal growth and spiritual development. She believes that mindfulness allows us to develop a deeper understanding of ourselves and our emotions, which is essential for self-awareness. Mindfulness also helps us to develop greater compassion and empathy towards ourselves and others, which is essential for building stronger relationships.

BK Sister Shivani emphasizes the importance of incorporating mindfulness into our daily lives. She suggests that we take a few minutes each day to practice mindfulness, whether it's through meditation, deep breathing, or simply paying attention to our thoughts and emotions. By making mindfulness a daily habit, we can begin to develop a greater sense of self-awareness and compassion towards ourselves and others.

## How self-awareness and mindfulness can positively impact our lives

Developing self-awareness and mindfulness can positively impact our lives in many ways. Here are some of the ways in which these practices can benefit us:

1. Improved relationships: When we are self-aware and mindful, we are better able to understand our emotions and communicate effectively with others. This leads to improved relationships with friends, family, and colleagues.

2. Better decision-making: Self-awareness allows us to make informed decisions about our lives. By understanding our strengths and weaknesses, we can make choices that align with our values and goals.

3. Reduced stress and anxiety: **Mindfulness has been shown to reduce stress and anxiety by helping us to stay present in the moment and not get caught up in negative thoughts.**

4. Increased empathy and compassion: **When we practice mindfulness, we develop greater empathy and compassion towards ourselves and others. This leads to stronger relationships and a greater sense of connection with the world around us.**

5. Greater sense of purpose: **Developing self-awareness and mindfulness can help us to better understand our values and goals, which can lead to a greater sense of purpose in life.**

6. Improved mental health: **Studies have shown that mindfulness can be an effective tool for managing depression and anxiety. It can also help to improve overall mental health and wellbeing.**

## Conclusion

Developing self-awareness and mindfulness is essential for personal growth and spiritual development. BK Sister Shivani's perspective on these practices emphasizes the importance of self-acceptance, compassion, and daily practice. By incorporating mindfulness and self-awareness into our daily lives, we can improve our relationships, make better decisions, reduce stress and anxiety, and develop a greater sense of purpose and wellbeing.

# Chapter 6. Letting Go of Negative Emotions and Cultivating Forgiveness

## Introduction

Negative emotions like anger, resentment, jealousy, and frustration can affect our mental and physical well-being. The inability to let go of these emotions can lead to stress, anxiety, and depression. Forgiveness, on the other hand, can bring peace, happiness, and healing. BK Sister Shivani is a spiritual teacher who has emphasized the importance of letting go of negative emotions and cultivating forgiveness. In this article, we will explore BK Sister Shivani's perspective on these topics and how they can benefit us in our daily lives.

## Understanding Negative Emotions

Negative emotions are a natural part of life, and we all experience them from time to time. However, holding onto these emotions can be detrimental to our well-being. BK Sister Shivani believes that negative emotions are a result of our expectations and attachment to things, people, or situations. When our expectations are not met, we feel angry, resentful, or frustrated. Similarly, when we are attached to something or someone, we fear losing them, which can lead to anxiety and stress.

BK Sister Shivani encourages us to understand the root cause of our negative emotions and to let go of our attachment and expectations. She teaches that we should focus on our inner state and not external factors. By doing so, we can cultivate a sense of detachment, which can help us overcome negative emotions.

## Letting Go of Negative Emotions

Letting go of negative emotions can be challenging, but it is essential for our mental and physical well-being. BK Sister Shivani suggests that we practice the following techniques to let go of negative emotions:

Acceptance: Accepting that negative emotions are a part of life and that we cannot control everything can help us let go of our attachment and expectations.

Mindfulness: **Practicing mindfulness can help us stay in the present moment and not dwell on past events or worry about the future.**

Gratitude: Cultivating a sense of gratitude can shift our focus from negative emotions to positive aspects of our lives.

Forgiveness: Forgiving ourselves and others can help us let go of anger, resentment, and other negative emotions.

## Cultivating Forgiveness

Forgiveness is an essential aspect of BK Sister Shivani's teachings. She believes that forgiveness is a powerful tool for healing and transformation. Forgiving ourselves and others can help us let go of negative emotions, which can lead to a more peaceful and fulfilling life. BK Sister Shivani suggests the following techniques for cultivating forgiveness:

1. Letting go of grudges: Holding onto grudges can cause us to become bitter and resentful. Letting go of grudges can help us free ourselves from negative emotions.

2. Empathy: Trying to understand the perspective of the person who has hurt us can help us cultivate empathy, which can lead to forgiveness.

3. Compassion: Cultivating compassion towards ourselves and others can help us let go of negative emotions and cultivate forgiveness.

4. Acceptance: Accepting that people make mistakes and that forgiveness is a process can help us let go of negative emotions and cultivate forgiveness.

# Benefits of Letting Go of Negative Emotions and Cultivating Forgiveness

Letting go of negative emotions and cultivating forgiveness can have several benefits. Some of the benefits include:

1. Improved Mental Health: Holding onto negative emotions can lead to stress, anxiety, and depression. Letting go of these emotions and cultivating forgiveness can improve our mental health and overall well-being.

2. Better Relationships: Forgiving ourselves and others can help us build better relationships with ourselves and others. We can learn to communicate better and develop empathy towards others.

3. Increased Happiness: Letting go of negative emotions and cultivating forgiveness can lead to increased happiness and fulfillment in life.

4. Inner Peace: Cultivating a sense of inner peace can help us cope with difficult situations and challenges in life. By letting go of negative emotions, we can find inner peace and calmness.

5. Spiritual Growth: BK Sister Shivani believes that letting go of negative emotions and cultivating forgiveness is an important part of spiritual growth. By doing so, we can connect with our inner selves and with a higher power, which can lead to a more fulfilling and purposeful life.

## Conclusion

Letting go of negative emotions and cultivating forgiveness is a process that requires practice and patience. BK Sister Shivani's teachings emphasize the importance of understanding the root cause of negative emotions and letting go of attachment and expectations. Forgiveness is a powerful tool for healing and transformation, and it can help us let go of negative emotions and cultivate a sense of inner peace and calmness. By practicing acceptance, mindfulness, gratitude, and compassion, we can let go of negative emotions and cultivate forgiveness, which can lead to improved mental health, better relationships, increased happiness, inner peace, and spiritual growth.

## Introduction

Spirituality has been a part of human history for thousands of years. It is the belief in a higher power, the interconnectedness of all beings, and the existence of a purpose beyond this physical realm. In recent years, there has been a growing interest in spirituality, particularly in the role it plays in inner transformation. BK Sister Shivani, a spiritual leader and a motivational speaker, has been at the forefront of this movement, sharing her insights on the importance of spirituality in achieving inner transformation.

## What is inner transformation?

Inner transformation is the process of changing one's inner world, thoughts, beliefs, emotions, and attitudes. It involves self-reflection, introspection, and a willingness to change. Inner transformation is not a one-time event but a continuous process that requires effort, commitment, and dedication. The goal of inner transformation is to develop a deeper understanding of oneself and the world around us and to live a more fulfilling life.

# The role of spirituality in inner transformation

BK Sister Shivani believes that spirituality plays a vital role in inner transformation. According to her, spirituality is the key to understanding oneself and the world around us. It helps us to connect with our inner self and find inner peace. Spirituality also helps us to develop a positive attitude towards life, to be more compassionate towards others, and to find meaning and purpose in our lives.

Here are some of the ways that spirituality can aid in inner transformation:

1. Developing self-awareness

Self-awareness is the foundation of inner transformation. It involves understanding one's thoughts, emotions, and behaviors. Spirituality helps in developing self-awareness by encouraging introspection and self-reflection. Through meditation, one can gain a deeper understanding of oneself and connect with one's inner self. This connection helps in developing self-awareness and a better understanding of one's thoughts, emotions, and behaviors.

## 2. Letting go of negative emotions

Negative emotions such as anger, fear, and anxiety can be detrimental to one's well-being. Spirituality provides a way to let go of these negative emotions and develop a more positive outlook towards life. By focusing on the present moment and letting go of past regrets or future worries, one can develop a sense of inner peace.

## 3. Developing compassion towards others

Spirituality helps in developing compassion towards others. By recognizing the interconnectedness of all beings, one can develop a sense of empathy and compassion towards others. This compassion helps in developing positive relationships and a sense of community.

Spirituality helps in finding meaning and purpose in life. By connecting with one's inner self and understanding one's values and beliefs, one can develop a sense of purpose. This purpose helps in guiding one's decisions and actions towards a fulfilling life.

# BK Sister Shivani's perspective on spirituality and inner transformation

BK Sister Shivani is a spiritual leader and a motivational speaker who has been spreading the message of spirituality and inner transformation for many years. According to her, spirituality is the key to achieving inner transformation. Here are some of her perspectives on the role of spirituality in inner transformation:

## 1. The importance of self-reflection

BK Sister Shivani emphasizes the importance of self-reflection in achieving inner transformation. According to hcr, self-reflection helps in developing self-awareness and a deeper understanding of oneself. She encourages her followers to take time for introspection and to ask themselves questions such as "Who am I?" and "What is my purpose in life?"

## 2. The power of thoughts

BK Sister Shivani believes that thoughts have the power to shape our reality. According to her, negative thoughts can create negative emotions, while positive thoughts can create positive emotions. She encourages her followers to focus on positive thoughts and to let go of negative thoughts.

## 3. The importance of meditation

Meditation plays a crucial role in achieving inner transformation, as it helps individuals develop a deeper connection with their inner selves and attain inner peace. According to her, meditation helps in calming the mind and developing a positive attitude towards life.

## 4. The interconnectedness of all beings

BK Sister Shivani emphasizes the interconnectedness of all beings. According to her, we are all connected and share a common destiny. She believes that recognizing this interconnectedness helps in developing compassion towards others and finding meaning and purpose in life.

### 5. The power of forgiveness

BK Sister Shivani believes in the power of forgiveness in achieving inner transformation. According to her, forgiveness helps in letting go of negative emotions and developing a sense of inner peace. She encourages her followers to practice forgiveness towards oneself and others.

### 6. The importance of service

BK Sister Shivani emphasizes the importance of service in achieving inner transformation. According to her, service helps in developing a sense of purpose and meaning in life. She encourages her followers to practice selfless service and to contribute to the betterment of society.

## Conclusion

Spirituality plays a vital role in achieving inner transformation. It helps in developing self-awareness, letting go of negative emotions, developing compassion towards others, finding meaning and purpose in life, and achieving inner peace. BK Sister Shivani's perspective on spirituality and inner transformation provides valuable insights into the importance of spirituality in achieving a fulfilling life. By incorporating spirituality into our lives, we can achieve inner transformation and live a more meaningful and fulfilling life.

# Chapter 8. Finding Purpose and Meaning in Life

## Introduction

Finding purpose and meaning in life can be a challenging task. It is something that we all strive for, yet it can seem elusive and unattainable. BK Sister Shivani, a spiritual teacher and motivational speaker, offers a unique perspective on how to find purpose and meaning in life.

BK Sister Shivani's teachings are rooted in the ancient Indian philosophy of Raj Yoga, which emphasizes the importance of connecting with the inner self to find peace and purpose. Her approach is practical, accessible, and relevant to people from all walks of life. In this article, we will explore BK Sister Shivani's perspective on finding purpose and meaning in life, and how her teachings can help us lead more fulfilling lives.

## The Inner Journey

BK Sister Shivani believes that the search for purpose and meaning begins with an inner journey. This journey involves introspection, self-awareness, and a deep connection with one's inner self. According to her, we are all spiritual beings having a human experience, and our true nature is divine. However, we often forget this truth as we get caught up in the distractions of daily life.

To connect with our inner self, BK Sister Shivani emphasizes the importance of meditation. Meditation allows us to quiet the mind, let go of our thoughts, and connect with our true nature. By meditating regularly, we can develop a deeper understanding of ourselves, our purpose, and our place in the world.

## Living with Purpose

Once we connect with our inner self, BK Sister Shivani believes that we can live with purpose and meaning. She emphasizes that our purpose in life is not something that we need to discover; it is something that we need to create. We can create our purpose by aligning our thoughts, words, and actions with our inner values and beliefs.

BK Sister Shivani suggests that we start by identifying our core values. What is most important to us? What do we believe in? Once we identify our values, we can begin to live in alignment with them. For example, if we value kindness, we can make a conscious effort to be kind to others. If we value honesty, we can strive to be truthful in all our interactions.

BK Sister Shivani also encourages us to focus on service. She believes that the purpose of life is not to accumulate wealth or material possessions, but to serve others. By serving others, we can make a positive impact on the world and find fulfillment in our lives.

## Overcoming Obstacles

Finding purpose and meaning in life is not always easy. We may face obstacles and challenges that make us question our path. According to BK Sister Shivani, these obstacles are a natural part of the journey, and we can overcome them by cultivating resilience and staying connected to our inner self.

One of the biggest obstacles we may face is fear. Fear can prevent us from taking risks and pursuing our dreams. BK Sister Shivani suggests that we overcome fear by focusing on love. Love is a powerful emotion that can help us overcome fear and find the courage to pursue our goals.

Another obstacle we may face is self-doubt. We may doubt our abilities, our worth, or our purpose in life. BK Sister Shivani encourages us to overcome self-doubt by cultivating self-love. Self-love involves accepting ourselves as we are, without judgment or criticism. By loving ourselves, we can build confidence and trust in our abilities.

## Living in the Present

BK Sister Shivani believes that finding purpose and meaning in life also involves living in the present moment. We cannot find fulfillment by constantly dwelling on the past or worrying about the future. Instead, we need to be fully present in the here and now.

Living in the present involves being mindful and aware of our thoughts, feelings, and surroundings. It means letting go of our worries and distractions and focusing on what is happening right now. By living in the present, we can experience life fully and find joy in the simple things.

BK Sister Shivani suggests that we cultivate mindfulness through meditation, deep breathing, and other mindfulness practices. By training our mind to focus on the present moment, we can reduce stress, increase our sense of well-being, and find greater meaning in life.

## Conclusion

BK Sister Shivani's perspective on finding purpose and meaning in life is grounded in the idea that we are all spiritual beings with a divine nature. By connecting with our inner self through meditation and introspection, we can create our purpose and live in alignment with our values and beliefs. We can overcome obstacles by cultivating resilience, love, and self-acceptance, and by staying pre sent in the moment, we can find fulfillment and joy in life.

BK Sister Shivani's teachings offer a practical and accessible approach to finding purpose and meaning in life. Her emphasis on spirituality, service, and mindfulness can help us lead more fulfilling lives and make a positive impact on the world around us. As we navigate the challenges and complexities of modern life, BK Sister Shivani's perspective can serve as a guiding light, helping us find our path and stay true to ourselves.

## Introduction

Self-realization is the process of discovering one's true self, beyond the surface-level identities and roles we play in society. It is a journey of self-discovery that requires a deep level of introspection and reflection. However, the path to self-realization is often fraught with obstacles and challenges that can make it difficult to stay the course. BK Sister Shivani, a spiritual leader and motivational speaker, offers a unique perspective on overcoming these obstacles and challenges on the path to self-realization.

### 1. Understanding the Nature of Obstacles

According to Sister Shivani, the first step in overcoming obstacles on the path to self-realization is to understand the nature of these obstacles. She explains that obstacles are not external circumstances or events but are internal thought patterns and belief systems that prevent us from realizing our true potential. These patterns can be deeply ingrained and can manifest as negative self-talk, limiting beliefs, and fears. Therefore, it is important to recognize these patterns and understand that they are not a reflection of our true selves.

## 2. Cultivating a Positive Mindset

One of the biggest obstacles on the path to self-realization is a negative mindset. Negative thoughts and emotions can hold us back from achieving our goals and can create a self-fulfilling cycle of failure. Sister Shivani emphasizes the importance of cultivating a positive mindset by focusing on gratitude, self-love, and positive affirmations. By replacing negative thoughts with positive ones, we can begin to shift our internal landscape and create a more positive and empowering mindset.

## 3. Embracing Change

Change is an inevitable part of life, and often the fear of change can prevent us from realizing our full potential. Sister Shivani explains that the key to overcoming this fear is to embrace change as a natural and necessary part of the self-realization process. By accepting that change is a necessary part of growth and expansion, we can begin to move forward with greater ease and confidence.

## 4. Practicing Mindfulness

Mindfulness is the practice of being fully present in the moment, without judgment or distraction. Sister Shivani explains that practicing mindfulness can be a powerful tool for overcoming obstacles on the path to self-realization. By focusing our attention on the present moment, we can begin to tune out the distractions and negative thought patterns that hold us back. Mindfulness also allows us to cultivate a greater sense of self-awareness and inner peace, which can be instrumental in overcoming obstacles and achieving our goals.

## 5. Connecting with a Higher Power

According to Sister Shivani, connecting with a higher power can be a powerful tool for overcoming obstacles on the path to self-realization. Whether through prayer, meditation, or other spiritual practices, connecting with a higher power can help us tap into a deeper sense of purpose and inner strength. By surrendering our fears and doubts to a higher power, we can begin to trust in the journey and overcome the obstacles that stand in our way.

Finally, Sister Shivani emphasizes the importance of finding support on the path to self-realization. Whether through friends, family, or spiritual communities, having a support system can be instrumental in helping us overcome obstacles and stay on track. Support can come in many forms, from words of encouragement to practical advice and guidance. By surrounding ourselves with positive influences and supportive people, we can begin to shift our internal landscape and create a more empowering and fulfilling life.

## Conclusion

The path to self-realization is a journey that requires courage, commitment, and perseverance. However, by understanding the nature of obstacles, cultivating a positive mindset, embracing change, practicing mindfulness, connecting with a higher power, and finding support, we can overcome the challenges that stand in our way and realize our full potential. BK Sister Shivani's perspective offers valuable insights and practices for anyone seeking to embark on this journey of self-discovery. By integrating these principles into our daily lives, we can begin to break free from limiting beliefs and thought patterns and create a more fulfilling and meaningful life. Self-realization is not a destination but a journey, and by embracing the obstacles and challenges along the way, we can emerge stronger, wiser, and more resilient than ever before.

# Chapter 10. The Importance of Self-care and Self-love

## Introduction

Self-care and self-love have become buzzwords in recent years, as more and more people are realizing the importance of taking care of themselves both physically and mentally. However, self-care and self-love are not just trendy concepts; they are essential practices that can significantly impact our overall well-being. BK Sister Shivani, an internationally renowned spiritual leader, has been advocating for the practice of self-care and self-love for many years. In this article, we will explore the importance of self-care and self-love from Sister Shivani's perspective and learn how we can incorporate these practices into our daily lives.

## What is Self-Care?

Self-care is any intentional activity that we engage in to take care of our physical, mental, and emotional health. It involves making conscious choices to prioritize our well-being and giving ourselves permission to rest, recharge, and rejuvenate. Self-care can take many forms, such as practicing yoga, meditating, taking a hot bath, reading a book, or spending time with loved ones. The key is to identify the activities that bring us joy and make us feel good and to make time for them regularly.

## Why is Self-Care Important?

Self-care is essential for several reasons. Firstly, it allows us to recharge and restore our energy levels, enabling us to function at our best. When we neglect self-care, we can quickly become exhausted and overwhelmed, leading to burnout and even physical and mental health problems. Taking time out for ourselves allows us to replenish our energy levels and recharge our batteries, so we can tackle challenges with renewed vigor.

Secondly, self-care can improve our overall well-being and reduce stress levels. Engaging in activities that bring us joy and make us feel good releases endorphins, which are natural stress-busters. When we make self-care a priority, we can reduce stress levels, improve our mood, and boost our overall health and well-being.

## What is Self-Love?

Self-love is the practice of treating ourselves with kindness, compassion, and acceptance. It involves recognizing our worth and value as individuals and embracing our strengths and weaknesses. Self-love is not about being self-centered or narcissistic; it is about learning to appreciate ourselves for who we are and treating ourselves with the same kindness and compassion that we show to others.

## Why is Self-Love Important?

Self-love is essential for several reasons. Firstly, it promotes mental and emotional well-being. When we love ourselves, we are less likely to engage in negative self-talk, self-sabotage, or self-destructive behaviors. We are more likely to make choices that serve our well-being and to set healthy boundaries in our relationships.

Secondly, self-love enhances our relationships with others. When we love ourselves, we are more capable of loving and accepting others for who they are. We are less likely to judge or criticize others and more likely to show compassion and understanding.

## Sister Shivani's Perspective on Self-Care and Self-Love

Sister Shivani, a spiritual leader and a well-known television personality, has been advocating for the practice of self-care and self-love for many years. She believes that self-care and self-love are not selfish practices but rather essential ones that enable us to live fulfilling and purposeful lives. Sister Shivani teaches that when we prioritize self-care and self-love, we can achieve greater levels of success, happiness, and inner peace.

According to Sister Shivani, self-care and self-love are interconnected practices. She believes that self-care is the foundation for self-love, and that by prioritizing self-care, we can learn to love ourselves more fully. Sister Shivani teaches that self-care involves taking care of our physical, mental, and emotional well-being and that we must make time for self-care regularly, just as we make time for our work, family, and other responsibilities. When we make self-care a priority, we can improve our health and well-being, reduce stress levels, and feel more energized and motivated.

Sister Shivani also teaches that self-love is an essential practice that enables us to live more fulfilling and purposeful lives. She believes that when we love ourselves, we are better able to love and accept others and to live in harmony with the world around us. Sister Shivani teaches that self-love involves accepting ourselves for who we are, recognizing our worth and value as individuals, and treating ourselves with kindness and compassion.

## How to Incorporate Self-Care and Self-Love into Your Daily Life

Incorporating self-care and self-love into your daily life does not have to be complicated or time-consuming. Here are some simple ways to prioritize self-care and self-love in your daily routine:

1. Make time for yourself - Set aside some time each day for activities that bring you joy and make you feel good. This could be anything from reading a book, taking a walk, practicing yoga, or simply relaxing and doing nothing.

2. Practice self-compassion - **Be** kind and compassionate to yourself, just as you would be to a dear friend. If you make a mistake or experience a setback, do not beat yourself up. Instead, treat yourself with kindness and understanding.

3. Practice gratitude - **Take** time each day to reflect on the things that you are grateful for in your life. Focusing on the positive can help shift your mindset and improve your overall well-being.

4. Set boundaries - **Learn** to say no to things that do not serve your well-being or align with your values. Setting boundaries can help you prioritize your needs and make time for self-care and self-love.

5. Connect with others - **Spend** time with people who lift you up and support your well-being. Building meaningful connections with others can improve your overall happiness and well-being.

## Conclusion

Self-care and self-love are essential practices that can significantly impact our overall well-being. By prioritizing self-care and self-love, we can improve our physical, mental, and emotional health, reduce stress levels, and live more fulfilling and purposeful lives. Sister Shivani's teachings on self-care and self-love remind us that these practices are not selfish but rather necessary for us to achieve greater levels of success, happiness, and inner peace. By incorporating self-care and self-love into our daily routines, we can improve our overall well-being and live more meaningful and fulfilling lives.

# Chapter 11. Building Harmonious Relationships with Others

## Introduction

In today's fast-paced world, where people are constantly juggling multiple responsibilities, maintaining harmonious relationships with others can be a challenging task. But, according to BK Sister Shivani, a spiritual leader and motivational speaker, building harmonious relationships with others is essential for leading a fulfilling life. In this article, we will explore BK Sister Shivani's perspective on building harmonious relationships with others and learn some practical tips to improve our relationships with others.

## Understanding the nature of relationships

According to BK Sister Shivani, relationships are not just about what we say or do but are primarily about how we think and feel about others. Our thoughts and feelings towards others create an energy field that can either attract or repel people. If we have positive thoughts and feelings towards others, we will attract positive relationships, and if we have negative thoughts and feelings towards others, we will attract negative relationships.

Therefore, BK Sister Shivani emphasizes the importance of cultivating positive thoughts and feelings towards others. She suggests that we should focus on the positive qualities of others and appreciate them for who they are. By doing so, we can create a positive energy field that attracts positive relationships into our lives.

## Developing empathy

Empathy is the ability to understand and share the feelings of others. According to BK Sister Shivani, empathy is an essential ingredient for building harmonious relationships with others. When we can empathize with others, we can understand their perspective and respond to them in a way that is respectful and compassionate.

To develop empathy, BK Sister Shivani suggests that we should put ourselves in the shoes of others and try to see the situation from their perspective. We should also listen actively to what others are saying and try to understand their emotions. By doing so, we can create a connection with others and build a foundation for a harmonious relationship.

## Effective communication

Effective communication is another critical factor in building harmonious relationships with others. According to BK Sister Shivani, communication is not just about what we say but also about how we say it. The tone of our voice, the words we choose, and our body language all play a crucial role in effective communication.

BK Sister Shivani suggests that we should communicate with others in a way that is respectful, clear, and compassionate. We should avoid using negative language, criticism, or blame and focus on expressing our feelings and needs in a non-threatening way. By doing so, we can create a safe and comfortable environment for open and honest communication.

# Forgiveness and Letting Go

Forgiveness is another important aspect of building harmonious relationships with others. Holding onto grudges and resentments can create negative energy that can damage relationships. According to BK Sister Shivani, forgiveness is not about condoning the other person's behavior but about letting go of the negative emotions that are holding us back.

To forgive others, BK Sister Shivani suggests that we should focus on the positive qualities of the other person and try to see the situation from their perspective. We should also practice self-forgiveness and let go of any negative emotions we may be holding onto.

## Practical Tips

Here are some practical tips suggested by BK Sister Shivani to build harmonious relationships with others:

> ❖ Practice daily meditation to cultivate a positive state of mind and reduce stress.

- ❖ Practice gratitude by focusing on the positive qualities of others and expressing appreciation for their contributions.
- ❖ Practice active listening by paying attention to what others are saying and responding in a way that shows understanding and empathy.
- ❖ Practice forgiveness by letting go of negative emotions and focusing on the positive qualities of others.
- ❖ Practice self-awareness by reflecting on our thoughts and feelings towards others and making conscious efforts to cultivate positive ones.

## Conclusion

Building harmonious relationships with others is an essential part of living a fulfilling life. BK Sister Shivani's perspective emphasizes the importance of cultivating positive thoughts and feelings towards others, developing empathy, effective communication, and forgiveness. By practicing these principles, we can create positive energy fields that attract positive relationships into our lives.

The practical tips suggested by BK Sister Shivani can be integrated into our daily lives to improve our relationships with others. It is essential to remember that building harmonious relationships is a continuous process that requires conscious effort and practice.

In today's world, where people are increasingly disconnected from each other, building harmonious relationships with others has become even more critical. By following BK Sister Shivani's perspective, we can create a world where people are connected, respectful, and compassionate towards each other, leading to a happier and more fulfilling life for all.

# Chapter 12. Integrating Spiritual Practices into Daily Life

## Introduction

In today's fast-paced world, where stress, anxiety, and uncertainty have become a part of everyday life, people are looking for ways to incorporate spiritual practices to find peace and inner calm. Spiritual practices help individuals connect with their inner selves and higher powers, which can lead to an improved sense of well-being and a more fulfilled life. BK Sister Shivani, a prominent spiritual leader, has been advocating the integration of spiritual practices into daily life to help individuals find meaning and purpose in their lives.

## Integrating spiritual practices into daily life

BK Sister Shivani believes that spiritual practices are not limited to prayer and meditation but can be integrated into every aspect of one's daily life. She believes that spirituality is not something that can be practiced only on special occasions or in specific settings. It is a way of life that must be incorporated into every action and thought.

The following are some of the key practices that BK Sister Shivani recommends for integrating spirituality into daily life:

## 1. Meditation and Reflection

Meditation is a powerful practice that helps individuals connect with their inner selves and higher powers. BK Sister Shivani emphasizes that meditation is not just a practice but a way of life. It can be done at any time, anywhere, and for any length of time. Even a few minutes of meditation each day can have a profound impact on one's sense of well-being.

Reflection is another important practice that BK Sister Shivani recommends. It involves taking a few minutes at the end of the day to reflect on one's actions, thoughts, and emotions. Reflection helps individuals understand their strengths and weaknesses and make necessary changes to improve their lives.

## 2. Mindful living

BK Sister Shivani emphasizes the importance of mindful living. Mindful living involves being fully present in the moment and paying attention to one's thoughts, emotions, and actions. It involves being aware of one's surroundings and being grateful for the little things in life. By practicing mindful living, individuals can reduce stress, increase focus, and improve their overall sense of well-being.

## 3. Service and compassion

BK Sister Shivani believes that service and compassion are essential aspects of spiritual practice. Service involves helping others without expecting anything in return. It is a selfless act that brings joy and fulfillment to both the giver and the receiver. Compassion involves understanding and empathizing with others, even in difficult situations. By practicing service and compassion, individuals can develop a deeper sense of connection with others and contribute to making the world a better place.

## 4. Positive thinking

BK Sister Shivani emphasizes the importance of positive thinking. Positive thinking involves focusing on the good in every situation and looking for opportunities for growth and learning. It involves replacing negative thoughts with positive ones and cultivating an attitude of gratitude. By practicing positive thinking, individuals can improve their mental and emotional well-being and attract positive experiences into their lives.

## 5. Self-awareness and self-reflection

BK Sister Shivani believes that self-awareness and self-reflection are essential for spiritual growth. Self-awareness involves understanding one's thoughts, emotions, and actions and how they affect oneself and others. Self-reflection involves taking time to examine one's beliefs and values and making necessary changes to align them with one's higher self. By practicing self-awareness and self-reflection, individuals can improve their relationships, make better decisions, and lead a more fulfilled life.

# Conclusion

Integrating spiritual practices into daily life is essential for finding inner peace and purpose in life. BK Sister Shivani's teachings emphasize that spirituality is not a separate practice but a way of life that can be integrated into every action and thought. By incorporating practices such as meditation, mindful living, service, positive thinking, and self-awareness into daily life, individuals can improve their sense of well-being, connect with their inner selves and higher powers, and lead a more fulfilled life.

In today's fast-paced and stressful world, taking time to integrate spiritual practices into daily life can seem challenging. However, BK Sister Shivani's teachings emphasize that even small steps towards spiritual growth can have a profound impact on one's life. By incorporating these practices into daily life, individuals can find inner peace and purpose, even amidst the chaos and uncertainties of life.

Overall, BK Sister Shivani's perspective on integrating spiritual practices into daily life provides valuable insights into the importance of spiritual growth and its impact on one's sense of well-being. Her teachings provide practical tools and guidance for individuals looking to incorporate spirituality into their daily lives and lead a more fulfilled life.

"Awakening Your Inner Self: Lessons from BK Sister Shivani's Inspirational Talks" is a comprehensive guide to inner transformation, drawing on the teachings and philosophy of the renowned spiritual leader, BK Sister Shivani. Through twelve chapters, the book covers a wide range of topics, including self-awareness, mindfulness, positive thinking, forgiveness, spirituality, purpose, and self-care, providing readers with practical tools and strategies for personal growth and development. With insights from BK Sister Shivani's perspective, this book offers a roadmap for anyone seeking to awaken their inner self and lead a more fulfilling life.

# ABOUT THE AUTHOR

**Mr. C. P. Kumar** is a retired Scientist 'G' from the National Institute of Hydrology, Roorkee, Uttarakhand, India. With a wealth of experience in his field, he has also been practicing alternative healing therapies for several years. He is skilled in Reiki Healing and Chakra Balancing with Pendulum Dowsing, and offers holistic therapy through Emotional Freedom Technique (EFT) for emotional issues. You can email Mr. Kumar at cpkumar@yahoo.com and also visit his Reiki blog at https://reiki-roorkee.blogspot.com/ for more information.

.